Everything Earthquakes and Tsunamis

Natural Disaster Books for Kids Grade 5 | Children's Earth Sciences Books

First Edition, 2020

Published in the United States by Speedy Publishing LLC, 40 E Main Street, Newark, Delaware 19711 USA.

© 2020 Baby Professor Books, an imprint of Speedy Publishing LLC

All rights reserved.

Without limiting the rights under the copyright reserved above, no part of this publication may be reproduced, stored in or introduced into a retrieval system, or transmitted, in any form, or by any means (electronic, mechanical, photocopying, recording, or otherwise), without the prior written permission of the copyright owner.

All images in this book have been reproduced with the knowledge and prior consent of the artists concerned, and no responsibility is accepted by producer, publisher, or printer for any infringement of copyright or otherwise arising from the contents of this publication.

Baby Professor Books are available at special discounts when purchased in bulk for industrial and sales-promotional use. For details contact our Special Sales Team at Speedy Publishing LLC, 40 E Main Street, Newark, Delaware 19711 USA. Telephone (888) 248-4521 Fax: (210) 519-4043.

10 9 8 7 6 * 5 4 3 2 1

Print Edition: 9781541960251
Digital Edition: 9781541963252

See the world in pictures. Build your knowledge in style.
www.speedypublishing.com

Table Of Contents

Earthquakes..7
Seismic Waves..15
Plate Tectonics..25
Measuring Earthquakes......................................43
Tsunamis...55
Summary..63

Earthquakes and tsunamis are very powerful and destructive forces of nature. In this book, you will learn all about earthquakes and tsunamis, how they start, why they happen, and how they work. Let's get started!

Earthquakes

SOME EARTHQUAKES CAN OPEN GIANT CRACKS IN THE GROUND.

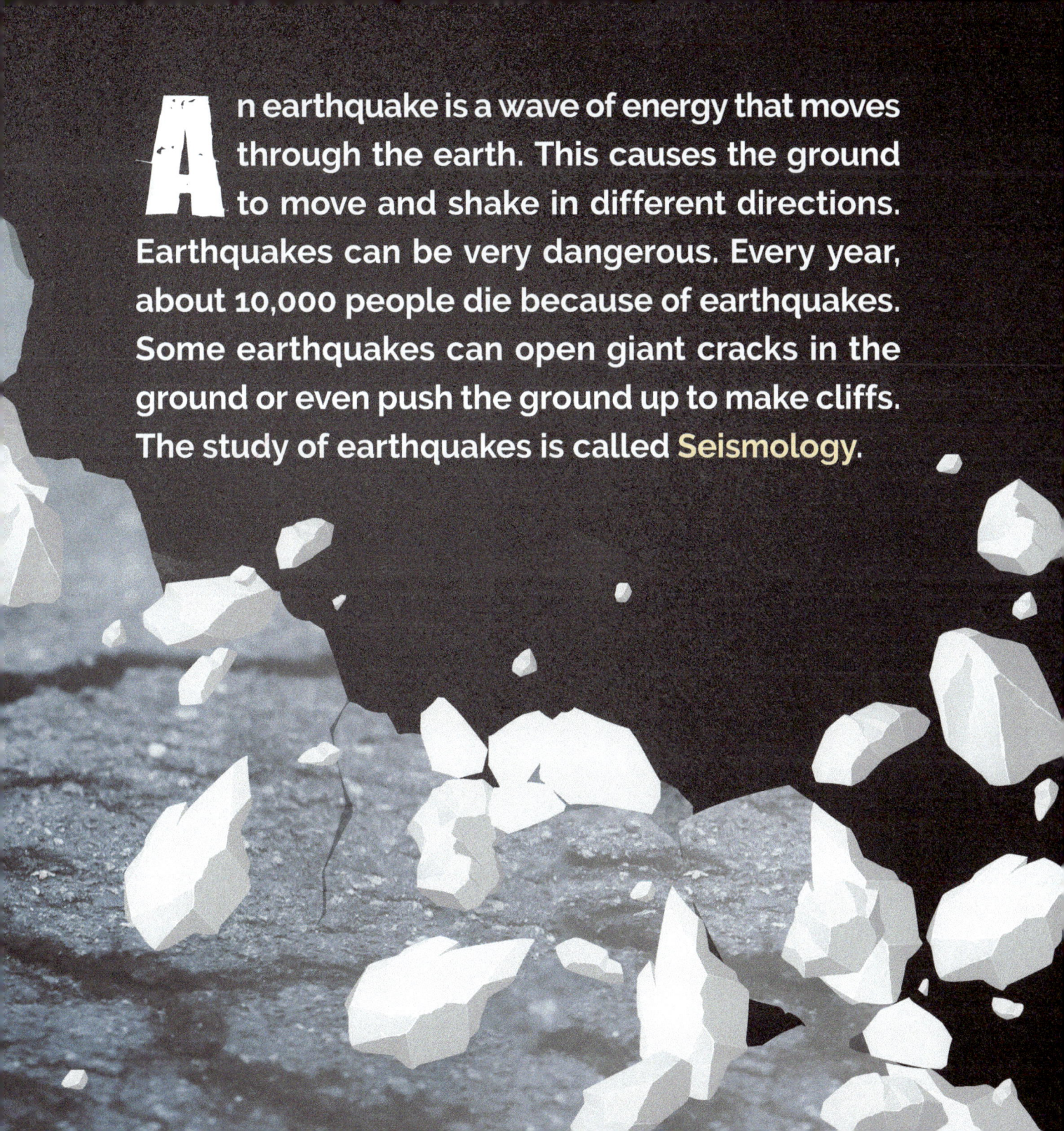

An earthquake is a wave of energy that moves through the earth. This causes the ground to move and shake in different directions. Earthquakes can be very dangerous. Every year, about 10,000 people die because of earthquakes. Some earthquakes can open giant cracks in the ground or even push the ground up to make cliffs. The study of earthquakes is called **Seismology**.

Some earthquakes are very small. **Temblors** are tiny earthquakes that happen all the time. They can't be felt by people, but they can be measured with special tools. **Tremors** are small earthquakes that you can feel. They are stronger than temblors but don't cause much damage. Tremors sometimes happen before a large earthquake.

TREMORS SOMETIMES HAPPEN BEFORE A LARGE EARTHQUAKE.

Major earthquakes are strong earthquakes that cause a lot of damage. They can knock down buildings and open cracks in the ground. **Great** earthquakes are the most powerful. These earthquakes are strong enough to destroy entire cities. Some great earthquakes are so strong that you can see the ground moving like a wave.

Seismic Waves

SEISMIC WAVES ARE LIKE THE RIPPLES CAUSED WHEN YOU DROPPED A ROCK INTO WATER.

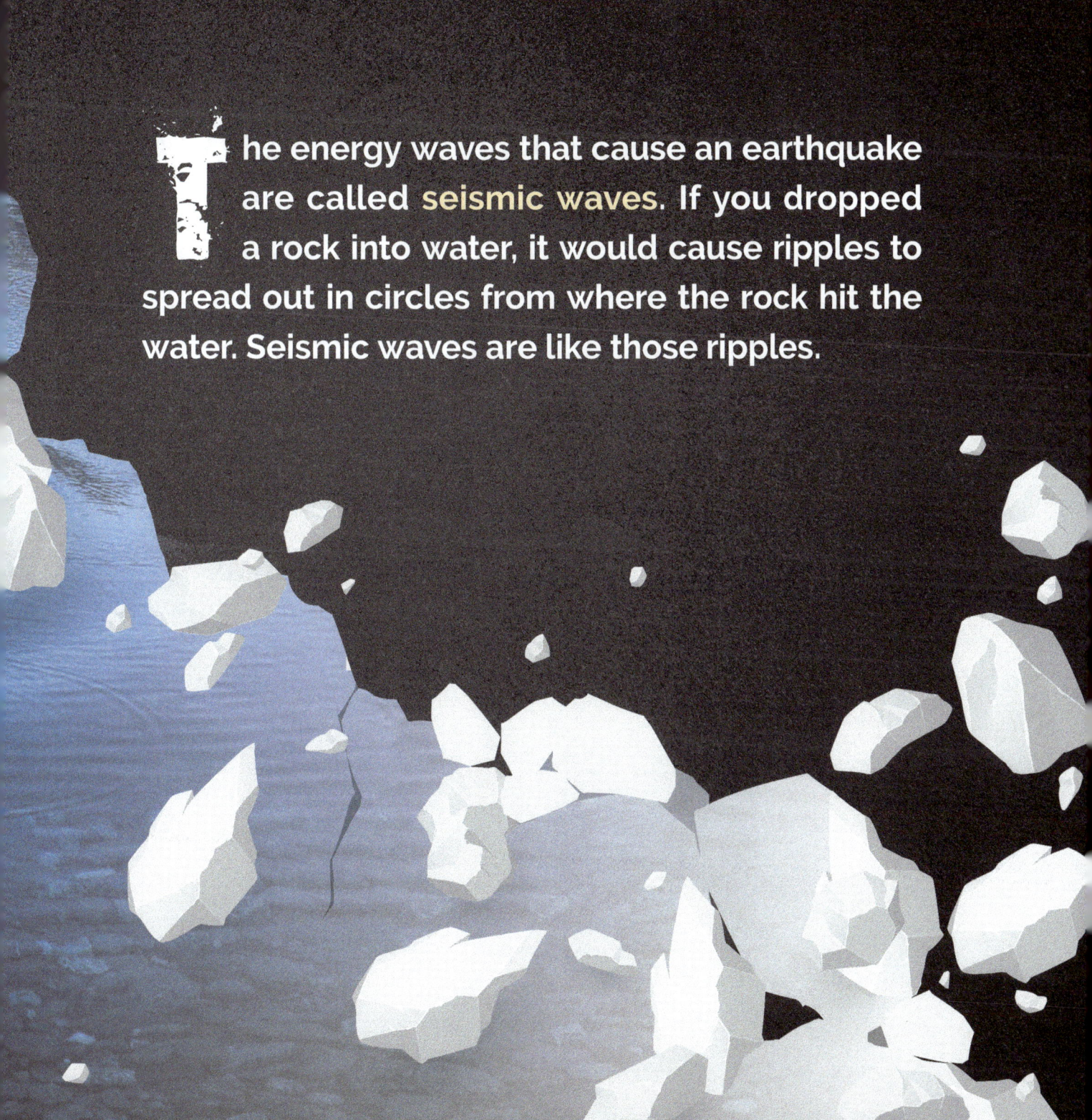

The energy waves that cause an earthquake are called seismic waves. If you dropped a rock into water, it would cause ripples to spread out in circles from where the rock hit the water. Seismic waves are like those ripples.

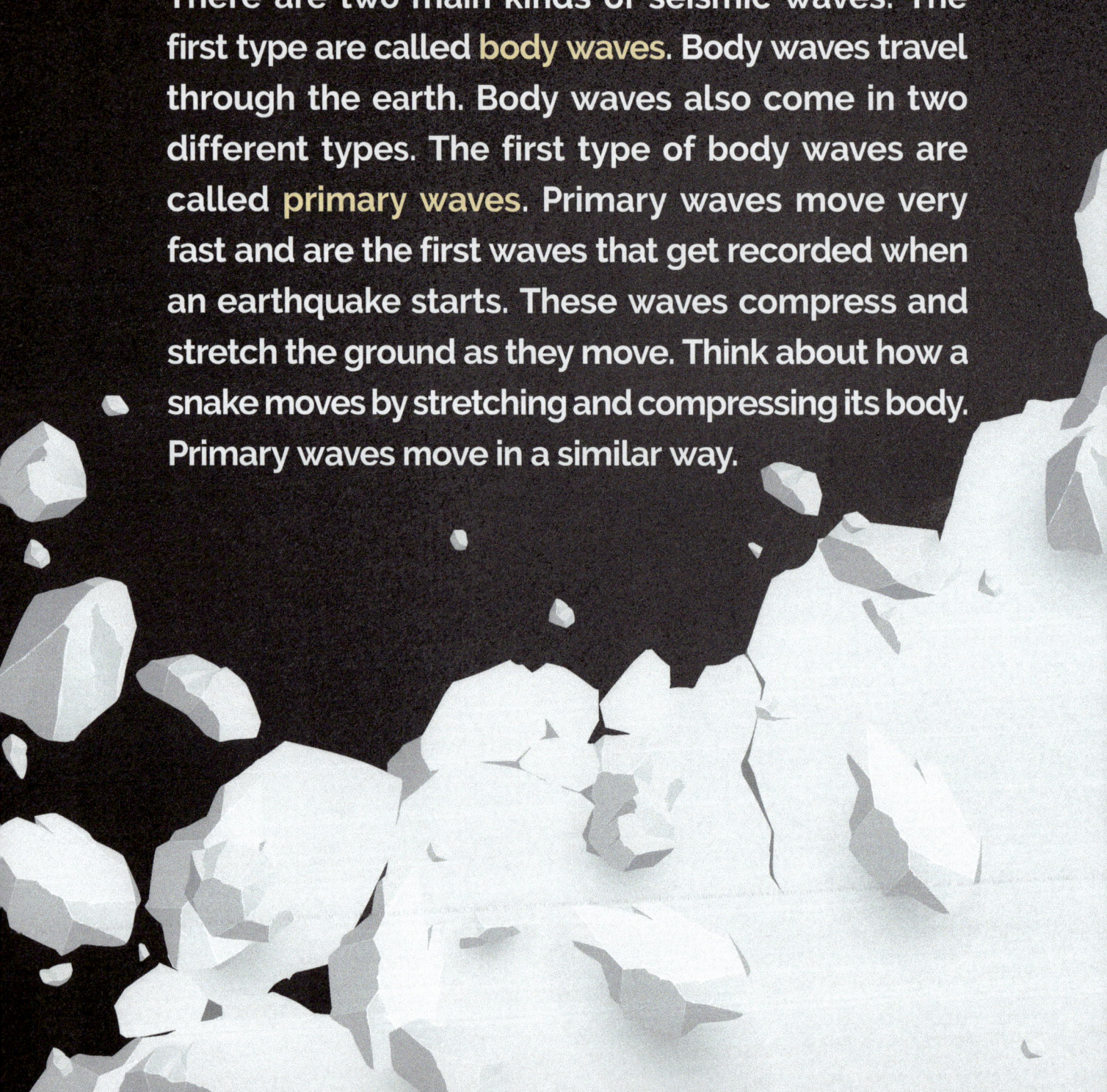

There are two main kinds of seismic waves. The first type are called body waves. Body waves travel through the earth. Body waves also come in two different types. The first type of body waves are called primary waves. Primary waves move very fast and are the first waves that get recorded when an earthquake starts. These waves compress and stretch the ground as they move. Think about how a snake moves by stretching and compressing its body. Primary waves move in a similar way.

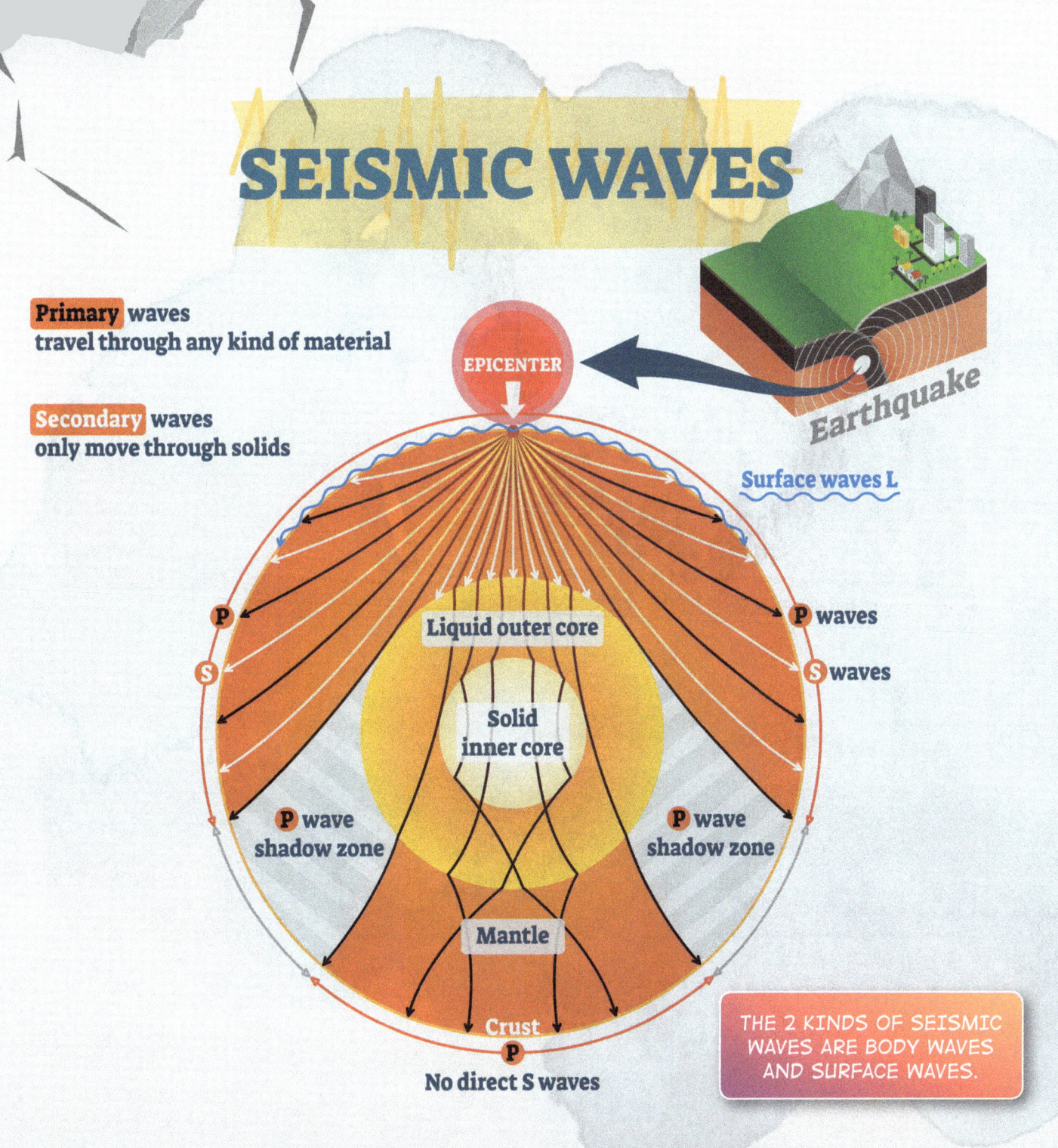

> THE 2 MAIN TYPES OF SURFACE WAVES ARE LOVE WAVES AND RAYLEIGH WAVES.

Surface wave comprising: Love wave — undisturbed rock

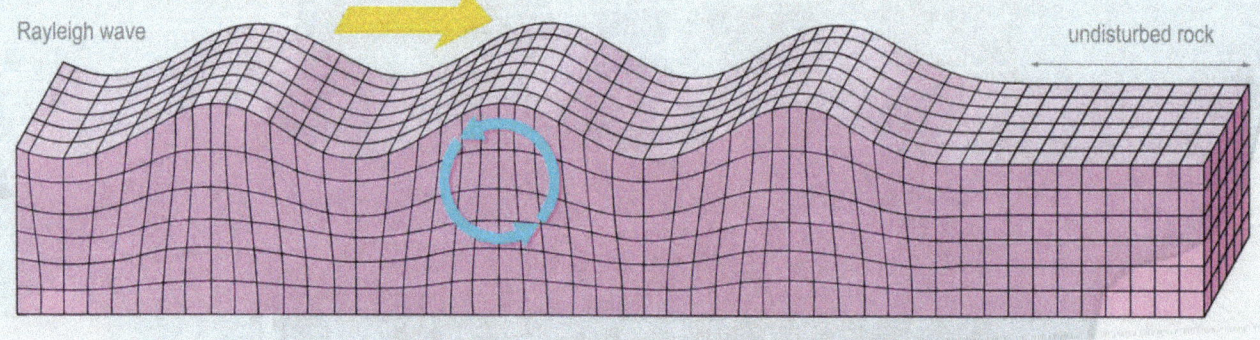

Rayleigh wave — undisturbed rock

The second type of body waves are called secondary waves. These waves move slower than primary waves. They also move up and down instead of straight like primary waves. As the waves move up and down, the ground also moves up and down.

Besides body waves, there are also surface waves. Surface waves move across the surface of the earth. These waves are the most dangerous and cause the most damage. Surface waves have two main types. Love waves move from side to side. Rayleigh waves move up and down and forward in a looping motion.

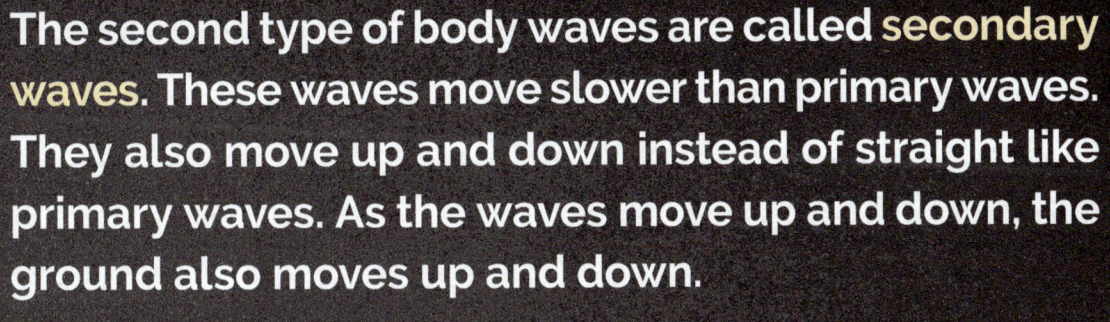

The **focus** of an earthquake is the place where the seismic waves start. Seismic waves move away from the focus in every direction at the same time like sound waves. Think about how you can hear someone talking even if they are above or below you. The spot on the surface of the ground right above the focus of an earthquake is called the **epicenter**. The epicenter is the place where surface waves spread out from like ripples in a pond.

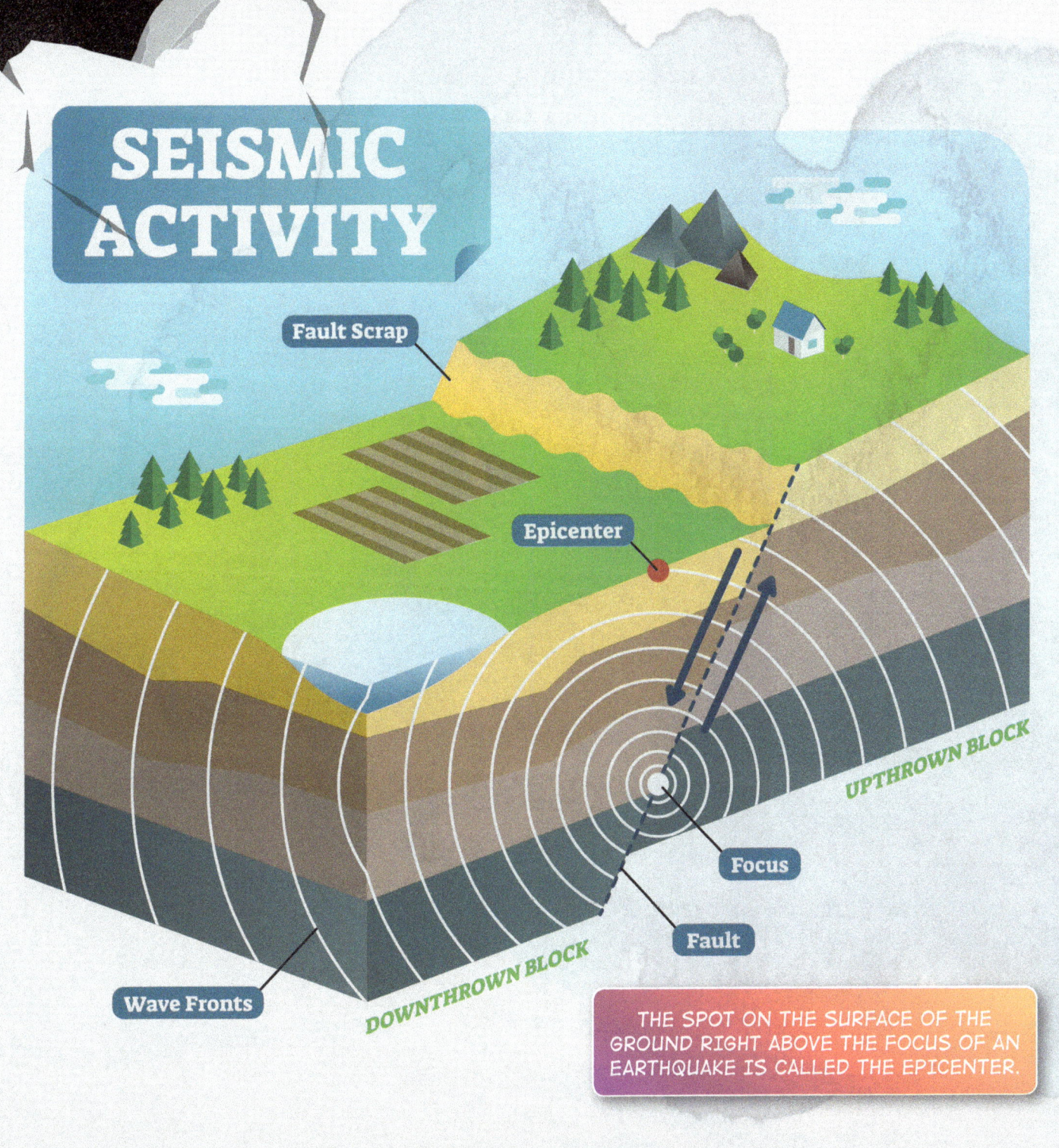

Plate Tectonics

TECTONIC PLATES OF PLANET EARTH

Tectonic plates are wide, thick chunks of rock that make up the earth's crust. They float on top of the mantle. The edge of a tectonic plate is called the plate boundary. Most earthquakes happen near plate boundaries because that is where two tectonic plates meet.

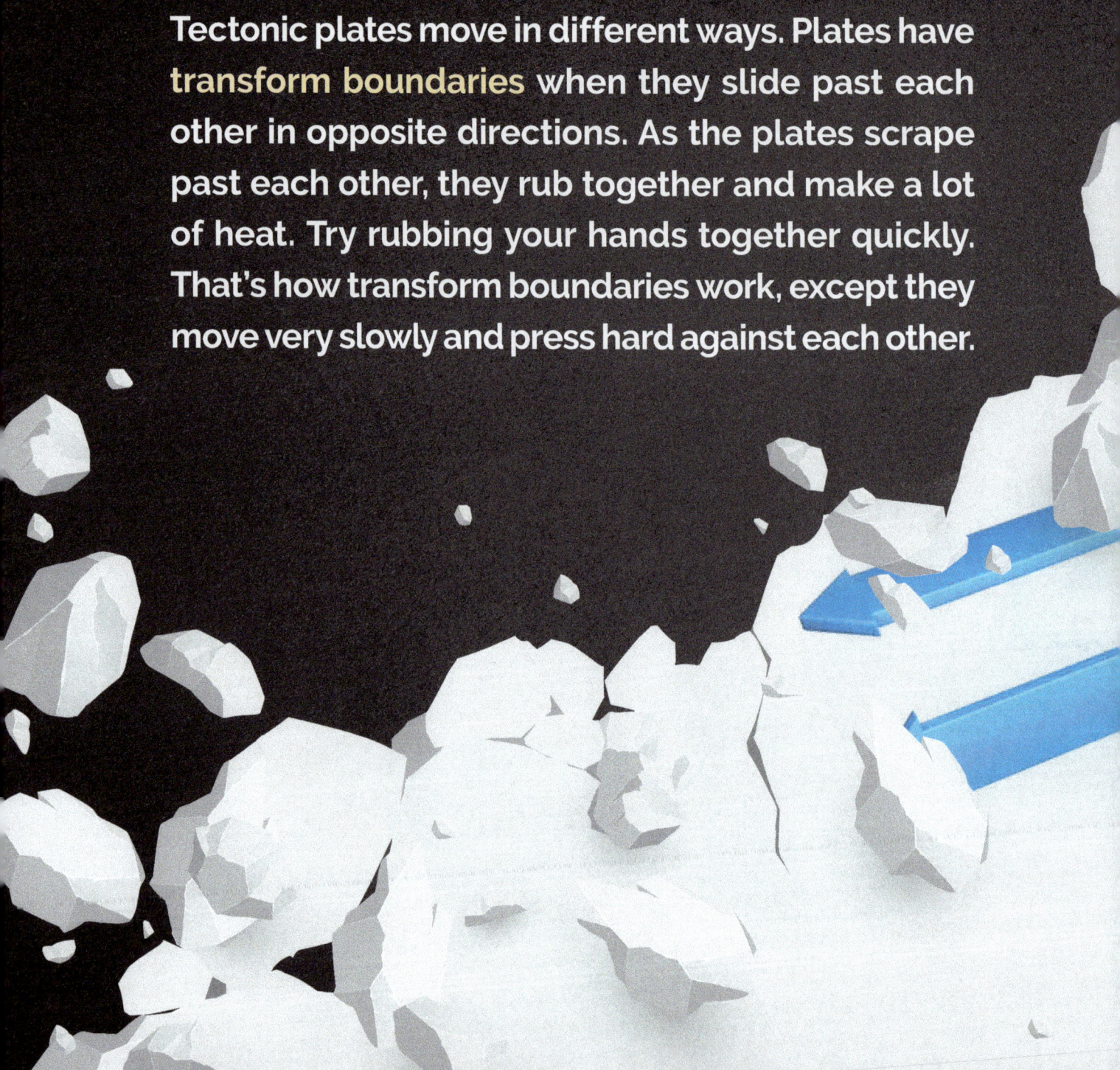

Tectonic plates move in different ways. Plates have **transform boundaries** when they slide past each other in opposite directions. As the plates scrape past each other, they rub together and make a lot of heat. Try rubbing your hands together quickly. That's how transform boundaries work, except they move very slowly and press hard against each other.

TRANSFORM BOUNDARIES

CONVERGING BOUNDARIES

When plates move toward each other, they have **converging boundaries**. Usually, when plates move toward each other, one of the plates gets pushed under the other. When this happens, it is called **subduction**. Strong earthquakes happen near places where plates have converging boundaries.

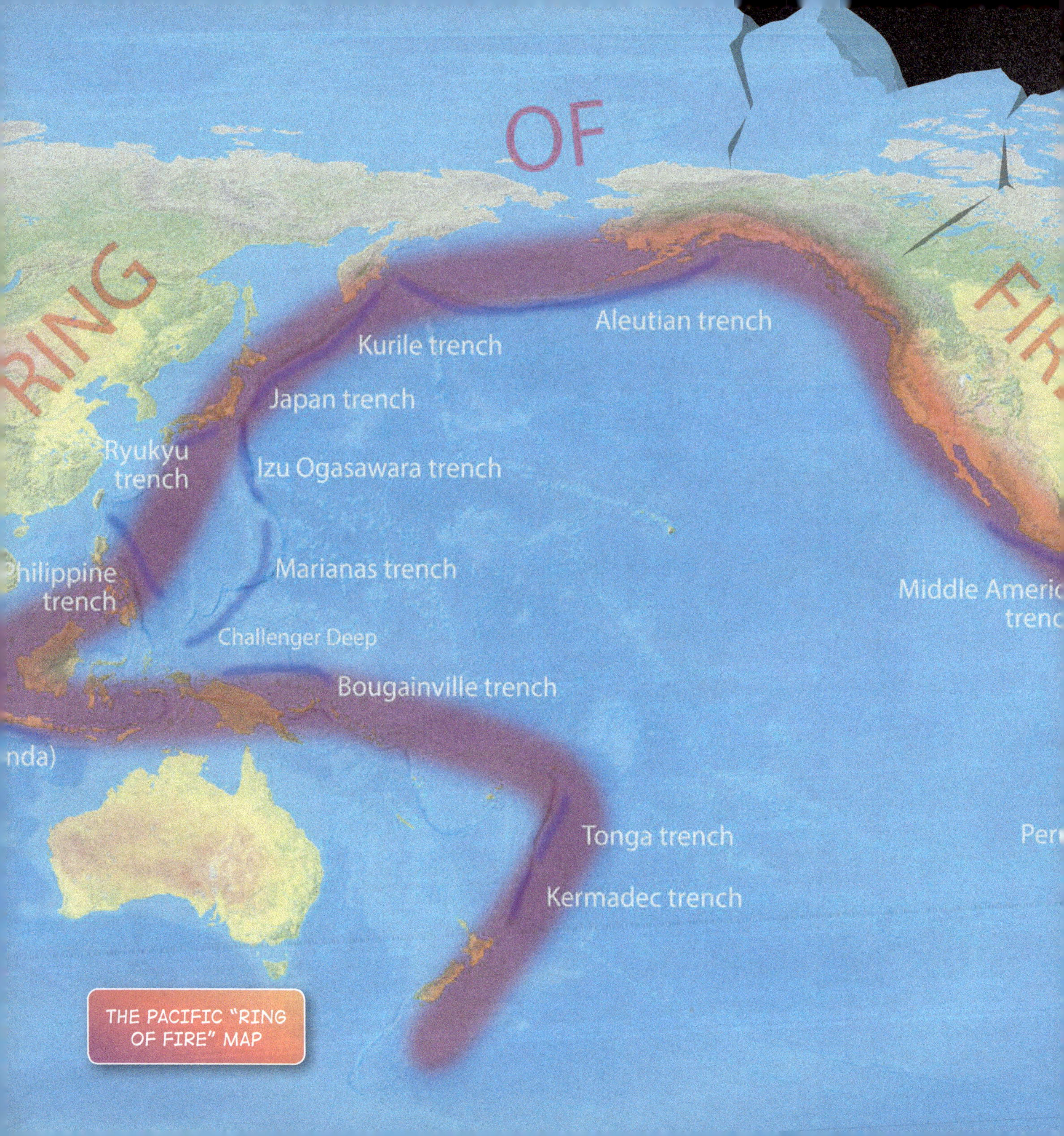

THE PACIFIC "RING OF FIRE" MAP

A famous subduction zone is called the Ring of Fire. Many strong earthquakes start there.

When two plates move away from each other, they have **diverging boundaries**. As the plates pull away from each other, magma comes up to the surface and hardens to fill in the gap.

DIVERGING BOUNDARIES

THE SAN ANDREAS FAULT IN THE CARRIZO PLAIN OF CALIFORNIA

Faults are lines that you can see on the surface of the ground above plate boundaries. The San Andreas Fault is a famous fault line.

The Mid-Atlantic Ridge is a 10,000 mile (16093.44 kilometer) long fault line on the bottom of the ocean! Many earthquakes happen near faults.

A BATHYMETRIC MAP OF THE MID-ATLANTIC RIDGE

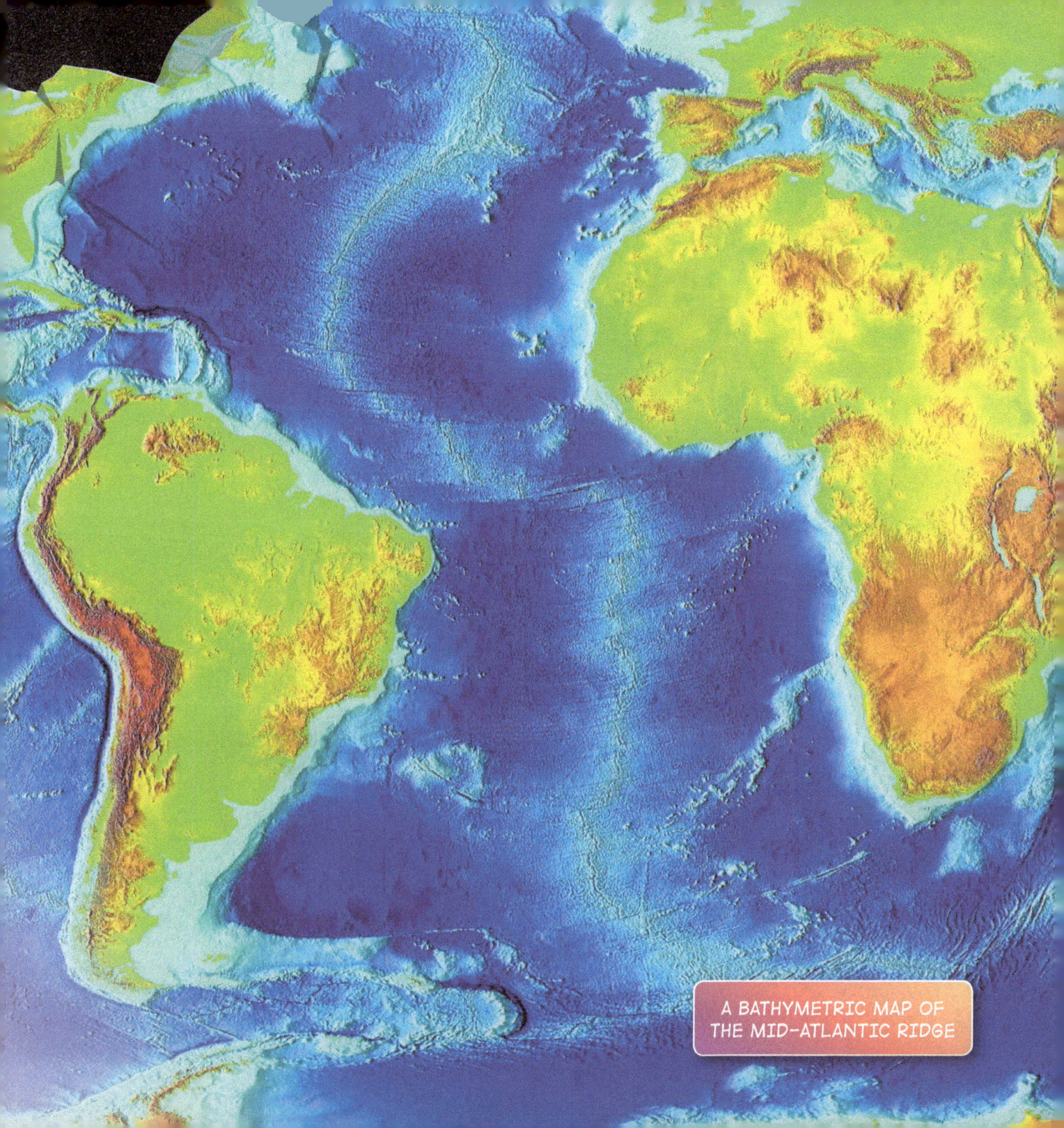

THE ENERGY THAT GETS RELEASED FROM THE MOVEMENT OF THE PLATES IS WHAT CAUSES AN EARTHQUAKE.

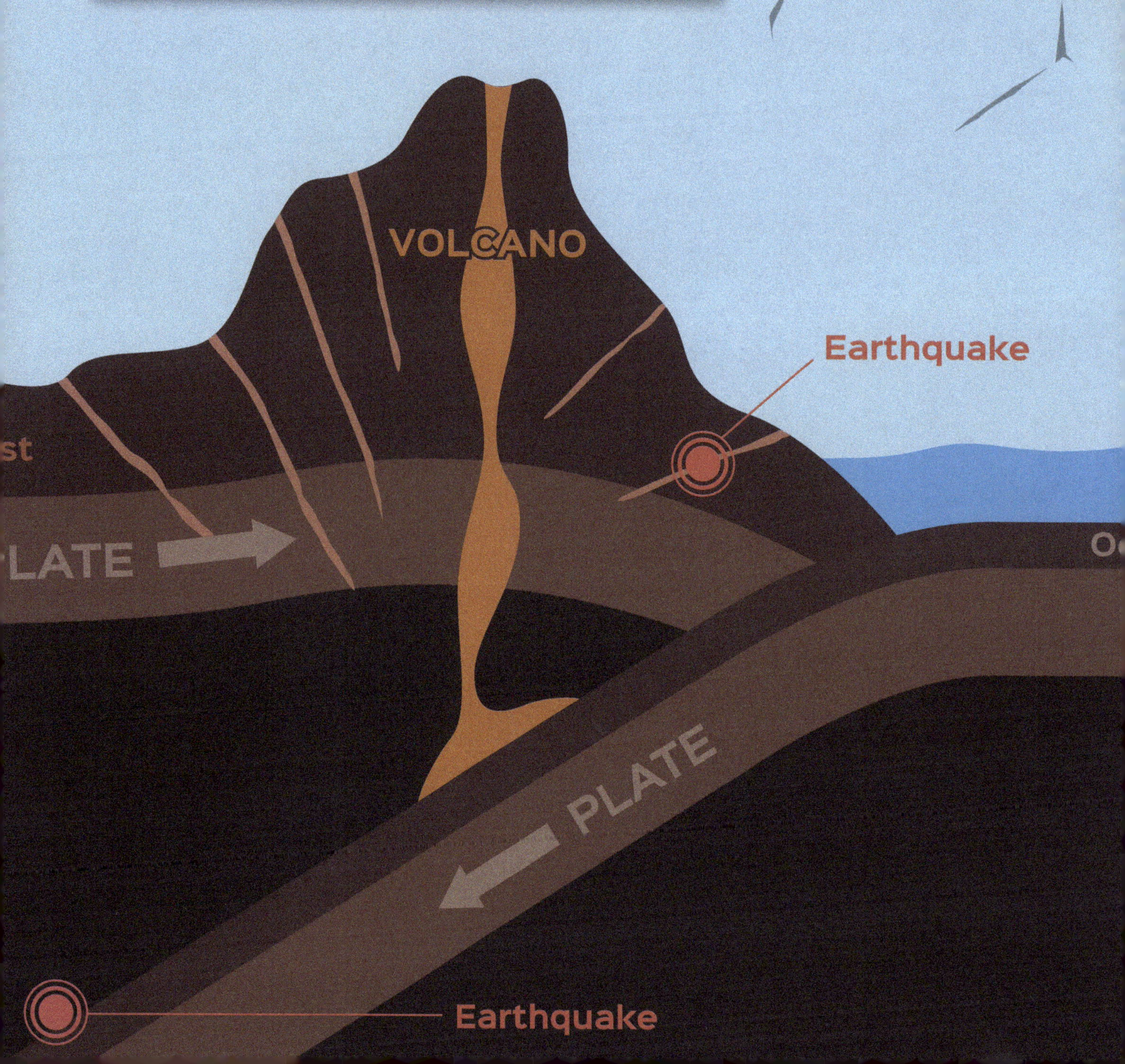

VOLCANO

PLATE

PLATE

Earthquake

Earthquake

As tectonic plates move past each other, they make a lot of heat. Sometimes parts of the plates will start to melt and stick together. Pressure starts to build up as the plates try to move. Eventually, the pressure builds up so high that the plates break apart and slide quickly past each other. The energy that gets released from this is what causes an earthquake. The place where the plates were stuck together is the focus of the earthquake.

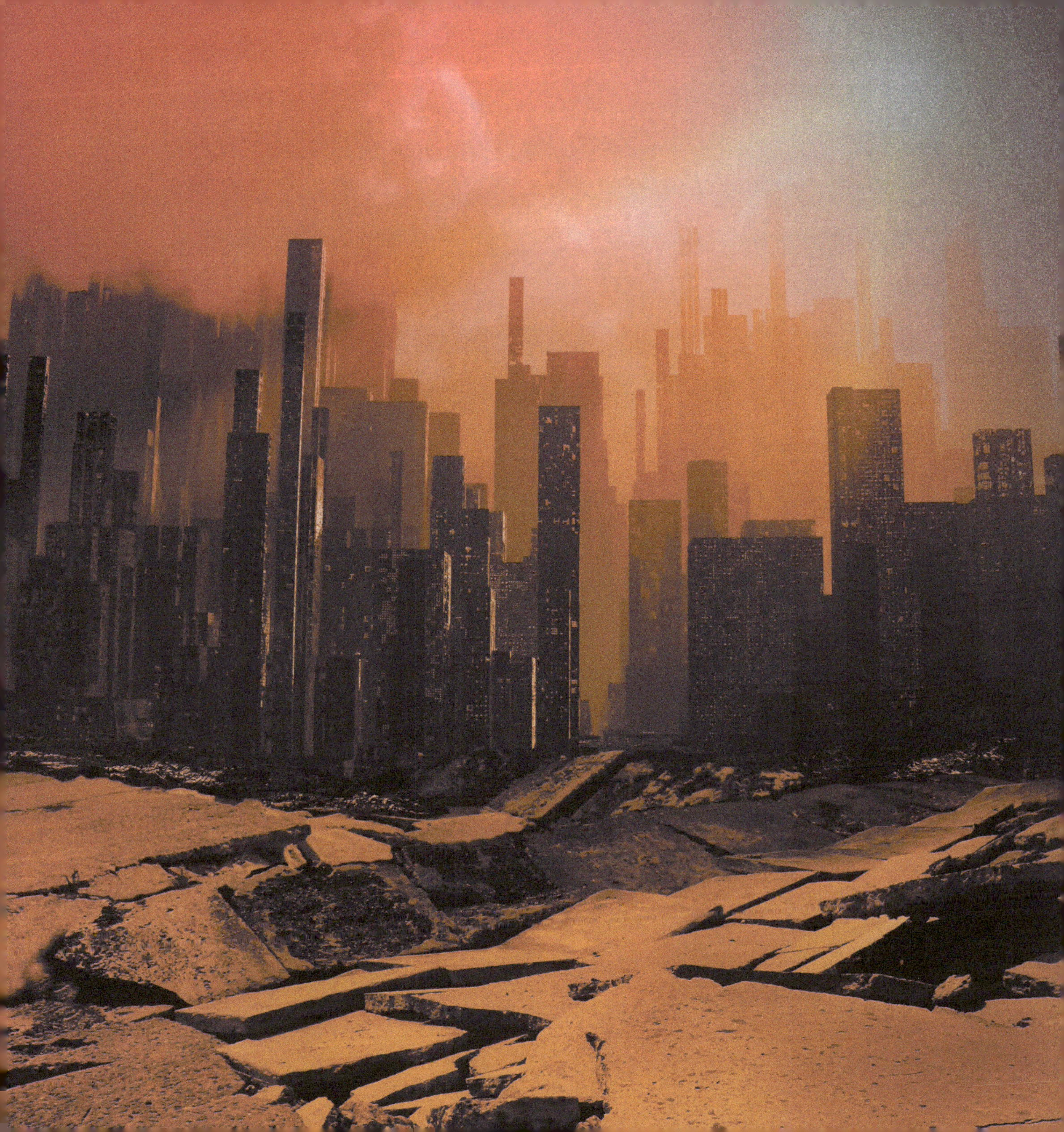

Measuring Earthquakes

SEISMOGRAPHS CAN PICK UP EVEN VERY SMALL EARTHQUAKES.

SEISMOGRAPH

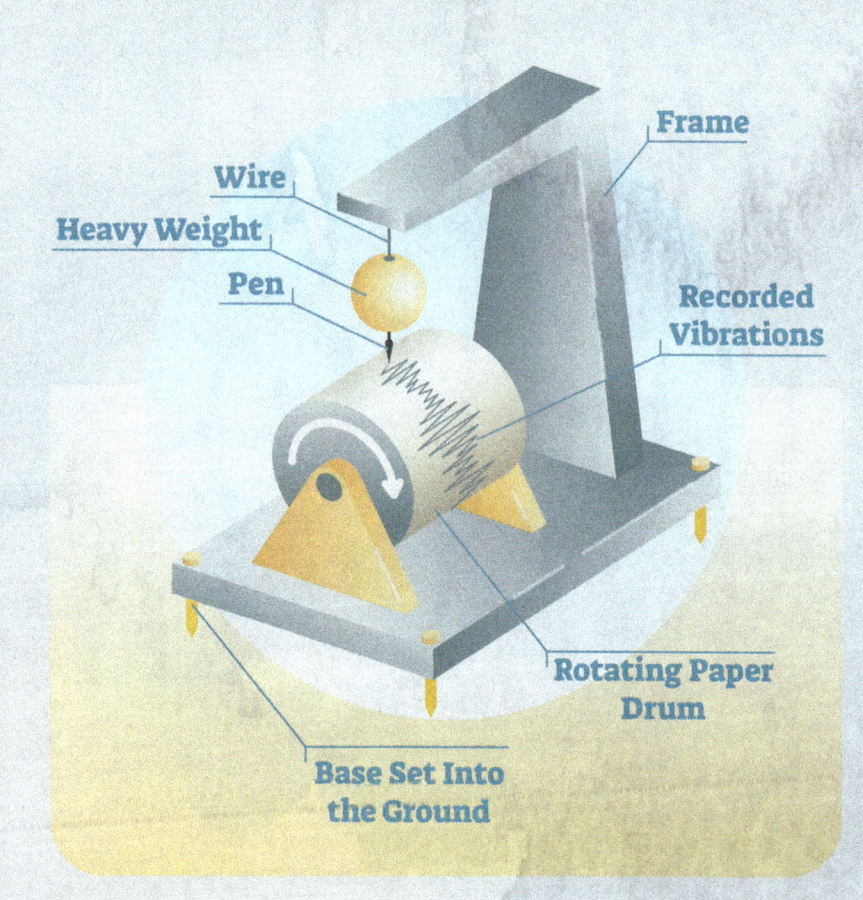

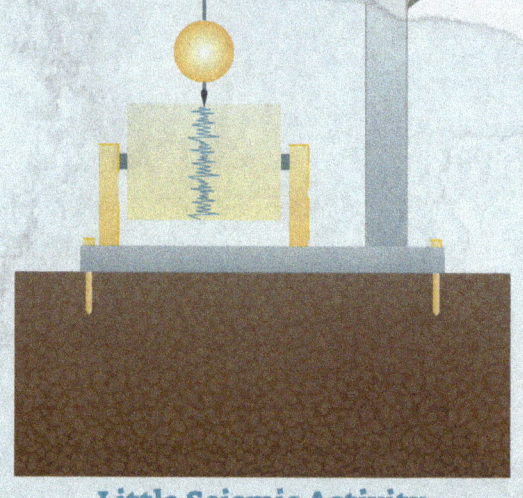

- Wire
- Heavy Weight
- Pen
- Frame
- Recorded Vibrations
- Rotating Paper Drum
- Base Set Into the Ground

Little Seismic Activity

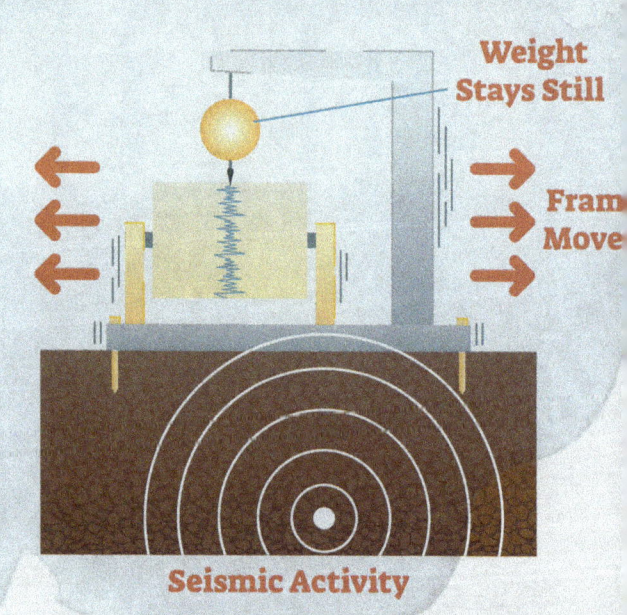

Seismic Activity
- Weight Stays Still
- Frame Moves

Today, earthquakes are measured by a machine called a seismograph. Seismographs can pick up even very small earthquakes. Seismologists put seismographs in places that have a lot of earthquakes.

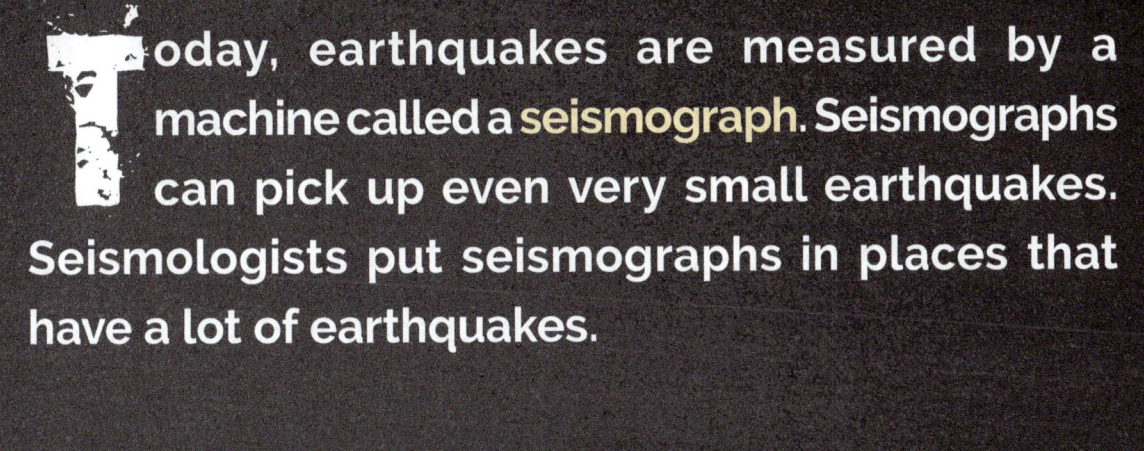

When an earthquake starts, a pen on the seismograph moves and makes marks on a piece of paper. Those marks show the strength of the earthquake, how long it lasted, and which direction it was moving in. Seismologists compare the readings from different seismographs to find out where the focus and epicenter of the earthquake was.

A PEN ON THE SEISMOGRAPH MOVES AND MAKES MARKS ON A PIECE OF PAPER WHEN AN EARTHQUAKE STARTS.

CHARLES FRANCIS RICHTER

GIUSEPPE MERCALLI

Two different types of measurements are used to see how strong an earthquake was. The Mercalli Scale and the Richter Scale. The Richter scale was invented in 1935 by Charles F. Richter. The Mercalli Scale was invented by Giuseppe Mercalli in 1902.

The Mercalli Scale is based on how much damage the earthquake caused. It starts at 1 and goes up to 12.

EARTHQUAKE MERCALLI INTENSITY

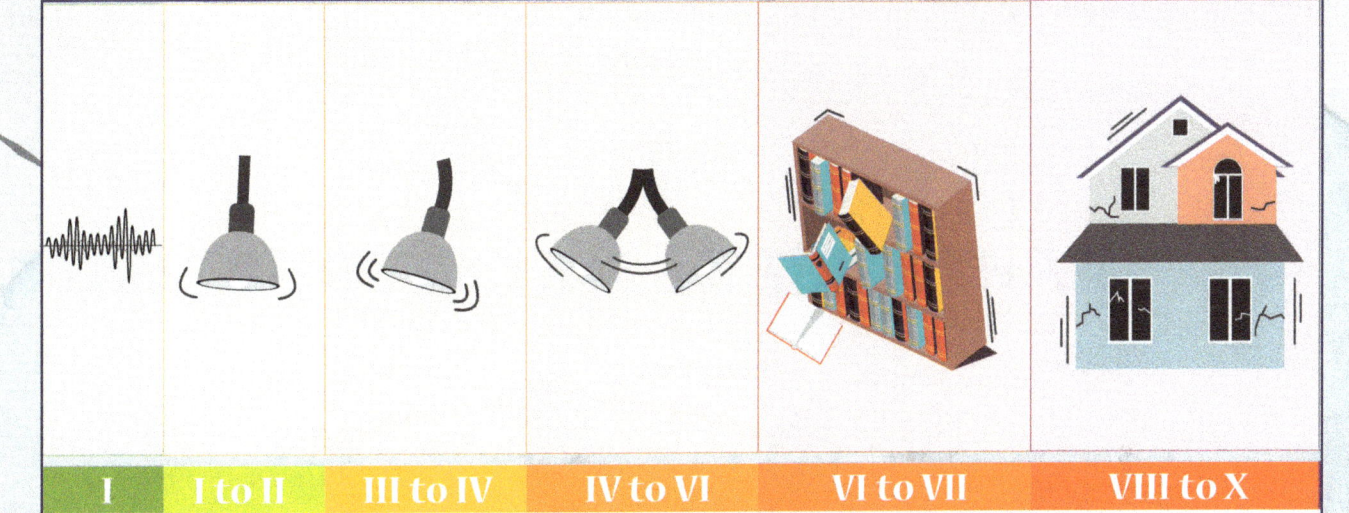

I	I to II	III to IV	IV to VI	VI to VII	VIII to X
not felt, but can be recorded by topography	Vibrations detected	Vibrations detected	Vibrations detected	Windows rattle or break, light damage	Crack in buildings, falling branches

X or great

buildings collapse, landslides   Devastation many deaths

THE MERCALLI SCALE

EARTHQUAKE MAGNITUDE SCALE

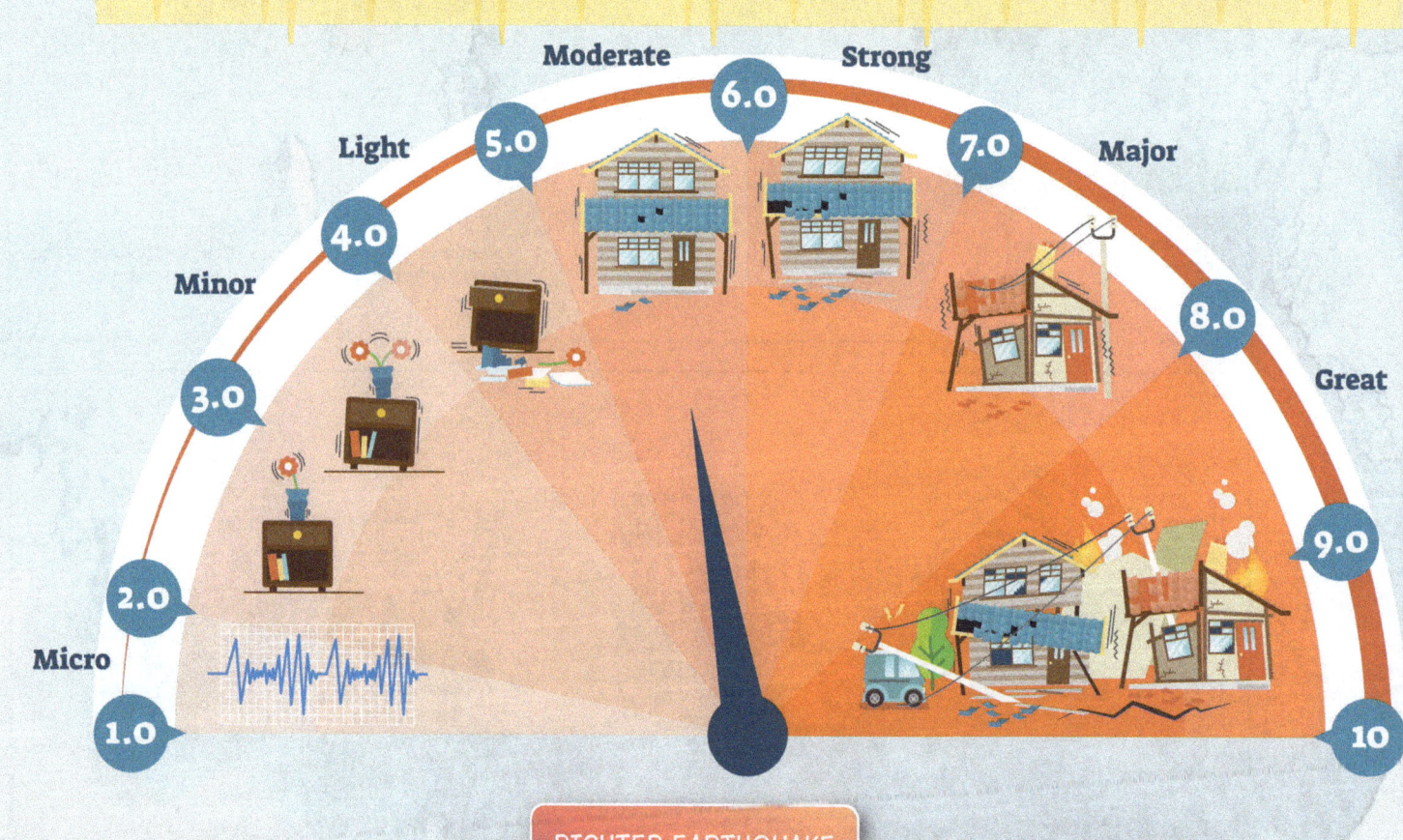

- Micro — 1.0
- Minor — 2.0, 3.0
- Light — 4.0
- Moderate — 5.0, 6.0
- Strong — 7.0
- Major — 8.0
- Great — 9.0, 10

RICHTER EARTHQUAKE MAGNITUDE SCALE AND CLASSES

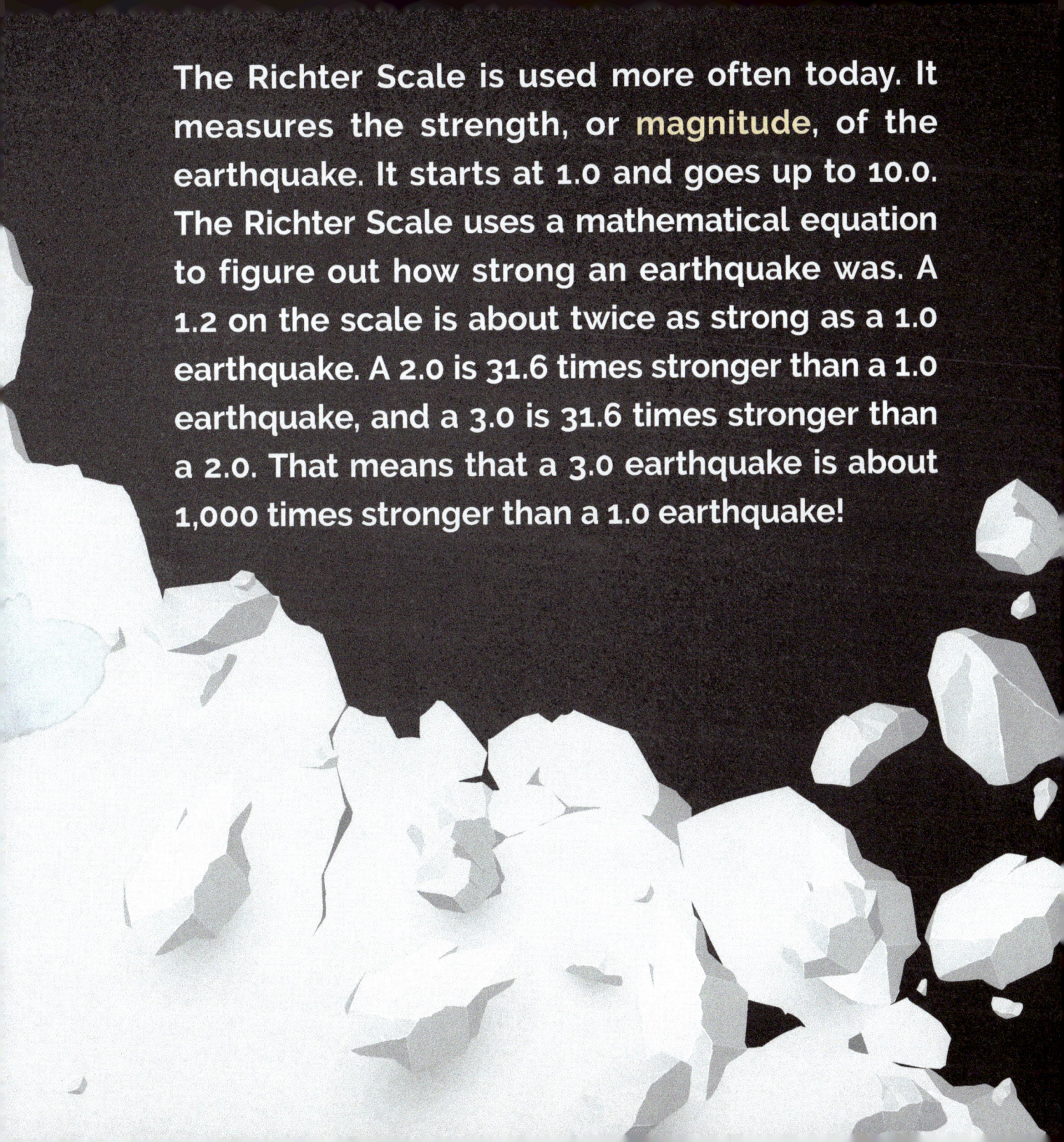

The Richter Scale is used more often today. It measures the strength, or magnitude, of the earthquake. It starts at 1.0 and goes up to 10.0. The Richter Scale uses a mathematical equation to figure out how strong an earthquake was. A 1.2 on the scale is about twice as strong as a 1.0 earthquake. A 2.0 is 31.6 times stronger than a 1.0 earthquake, and a 3.0 is 31.6 times stronger than a 2.0. That means that a 3.0 earthquake is about 1,000 times stronger than a 1.0 earthquake!

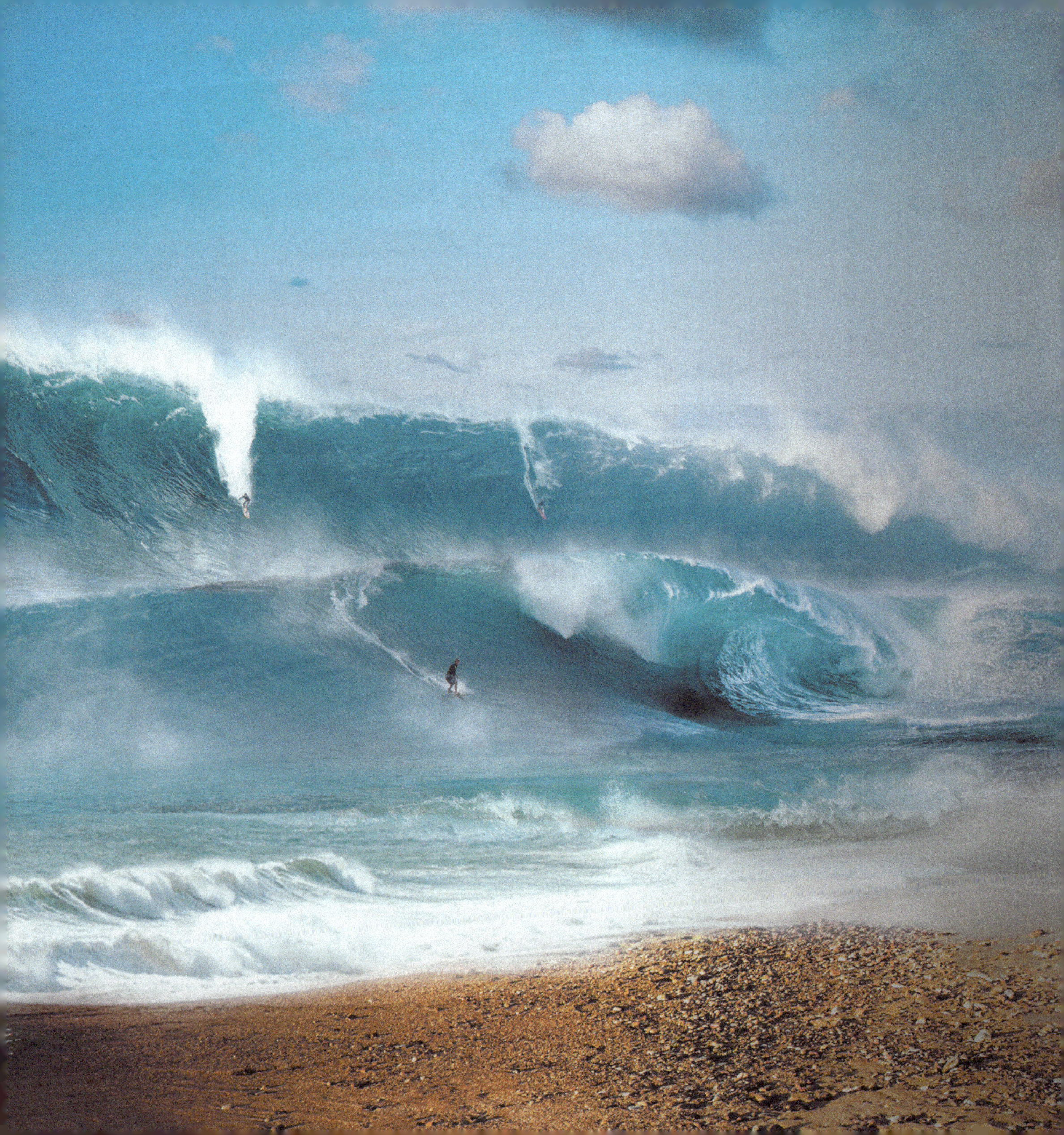

Tsunamis

Tsunami infographic

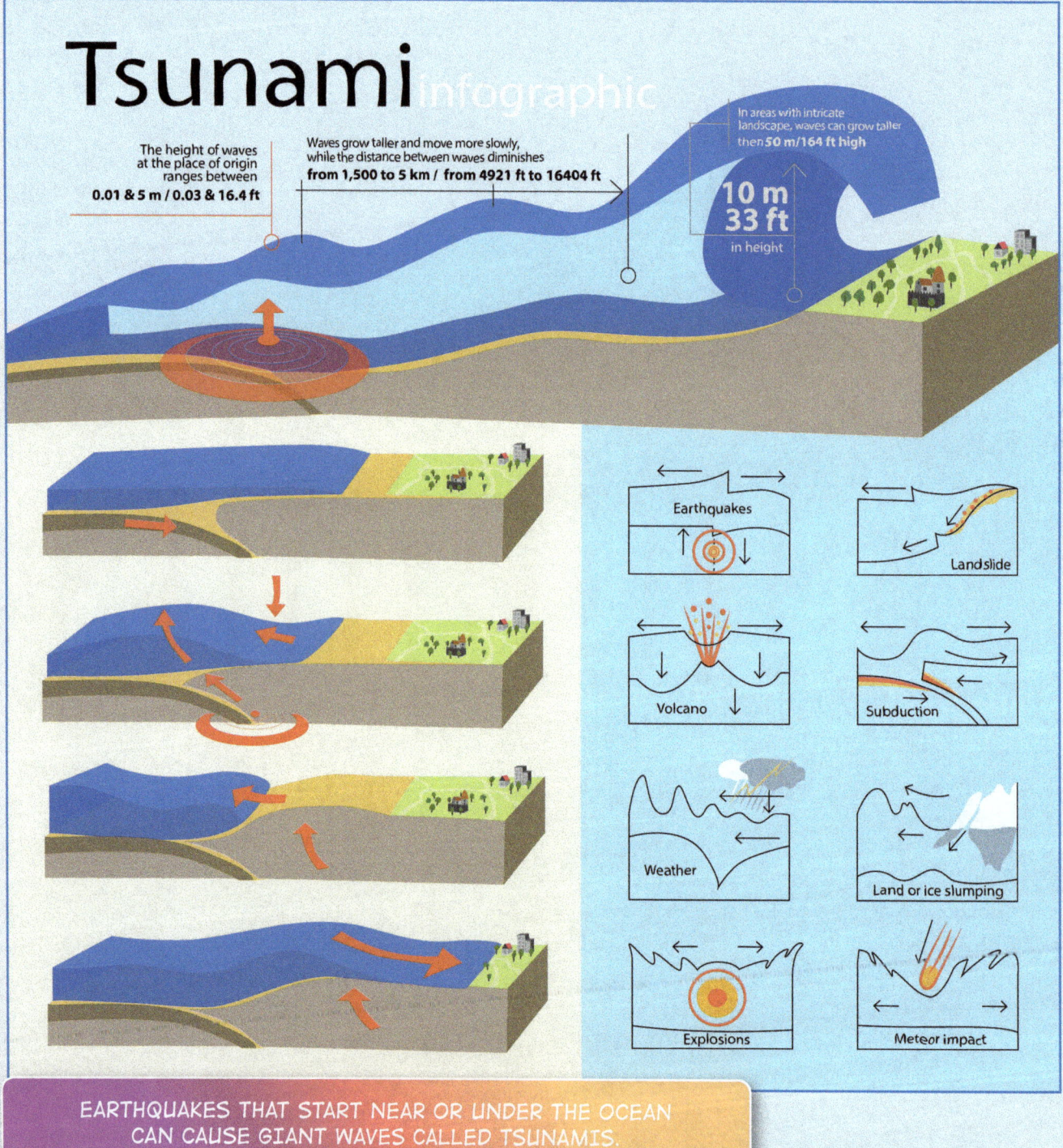

The height of waves at the place of origin ranges between **0.01 & 5 m / 0.03 & 16.4 ft**

Waves grow taller and move more slowly, while the distance between waves diminishes **from 1,500 to 5 km / from 4921 ft to 16404 ft**

In areas with intricate landscape, waves can grow taller then **50 m/164 ft high**

10 m / 33 ft in height

- Earthquakes
- Landslide
- Volcano
- Subduction
- Weather
- Land or ice slumping
- Explosions
- Meteor impact

EARTHQUAKES THAT START NEAR OR UNDER THE OCEAN CAN CAUSE GIANT WAVES CALLED TSUNAMIS.

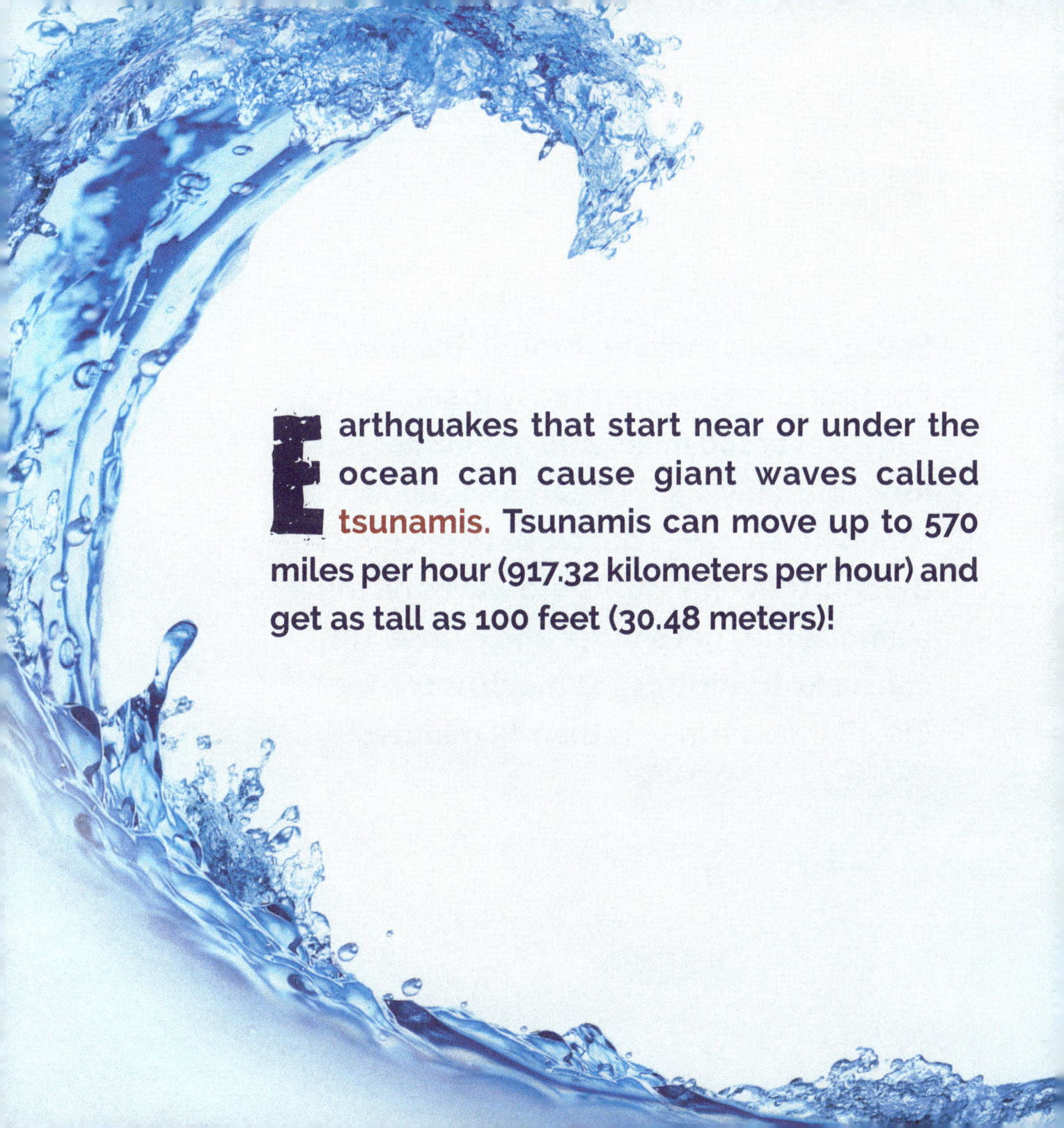

Earthquakes that start near or under the ocean can cause giant waves called **tsunamis.** Tsunamis can move up to 570 miles per hour (917.32 kilometers per hour) and get as tall as 100 feet (30.48 meters)!

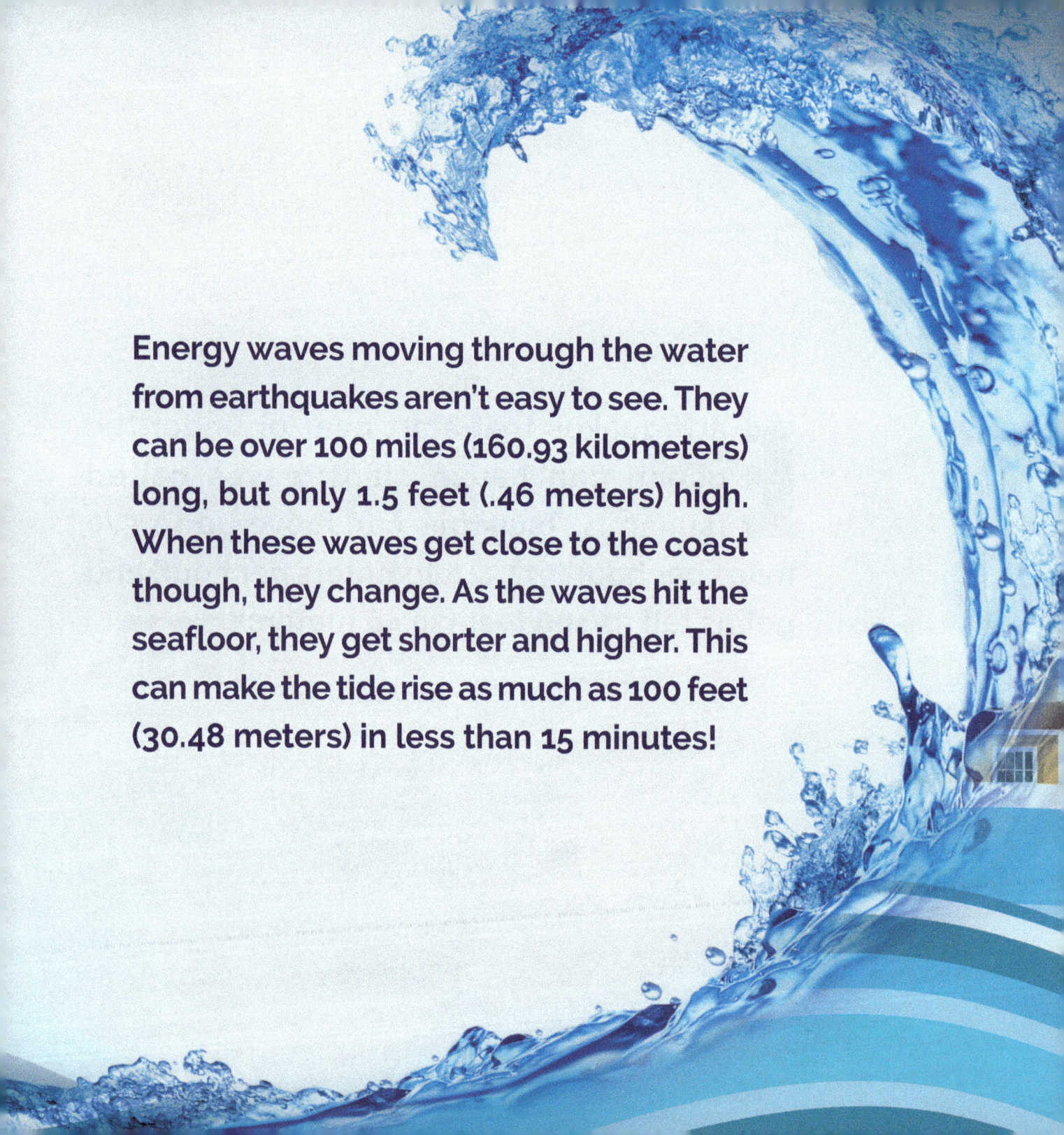

Energy waves moving through the water from earthquakes aren't easy to see. They can be over 100 miles (160.93 kilometers) long, but only 1.5 feet (.46 meters) high. When these waves get close to the coast though, they change. As the waves hit the seafloor, they get shorter and higher. This can make the tide rise as much as 100 feet (30.48 meters) in less than 15 minutes!

ENERGY WAVES MOVING THROUGH THE WATER FROM EARTHQUAKES AREN'T EASY TO SEE.

RUN-UPS ARE WAVES THAT MOVE FAR INLAND AND RIP UP TREES, KNOCK DOWN BUILDINGS, AND FLOOD EVERYTHING.

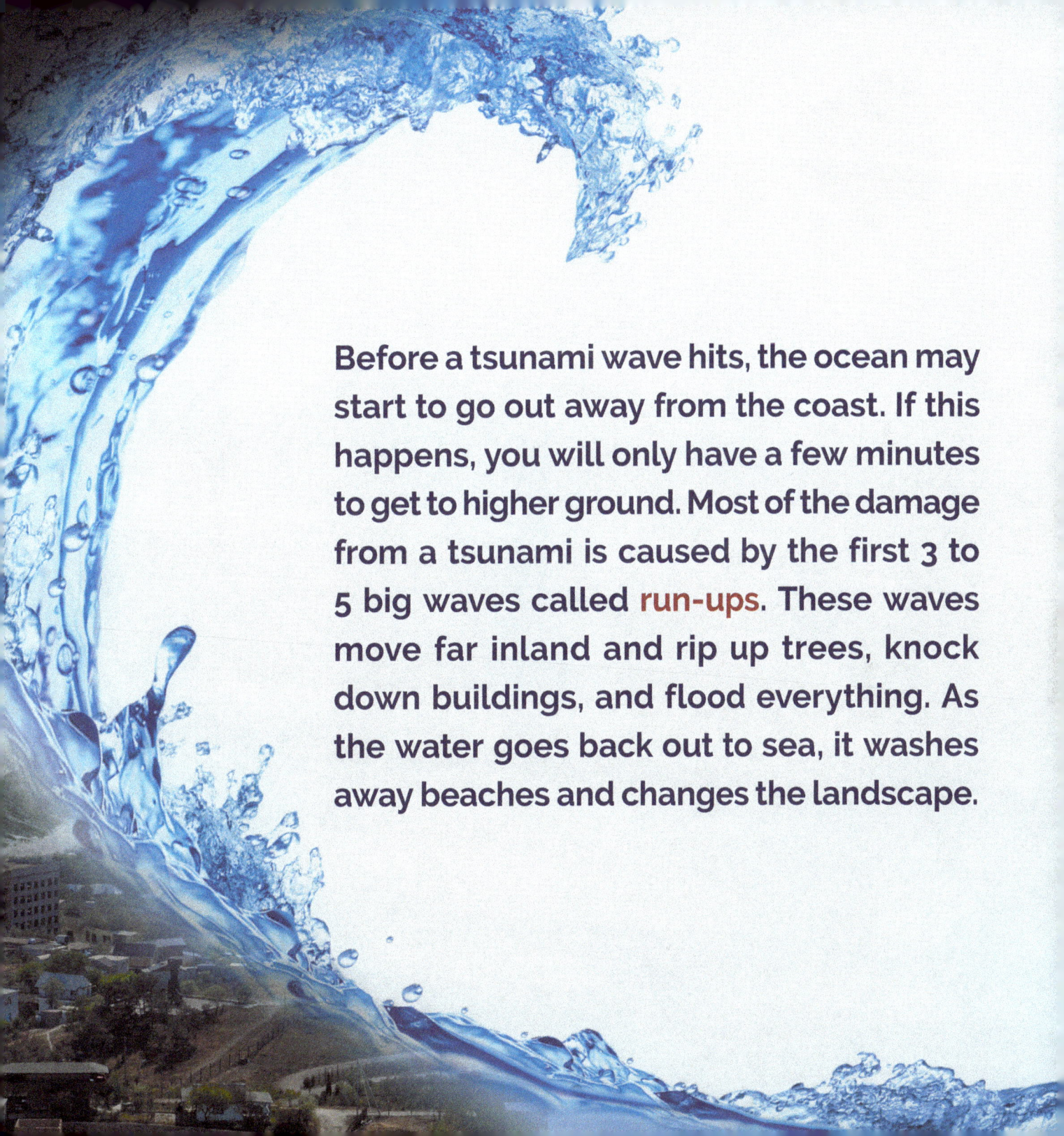

Before a tsunami wave hits, the ocean may start to go out away from the coast. If this happens, you will only have a few minutes to get to higher ground. Most of the damage from a tsunami is caused by the first 3 to 5 big waves called **run-ups**. These waves move far inland and rip up trees, knock down buildings, and flood everything. As the water goes back out to sea, it washes away beaches and changes the landscape.

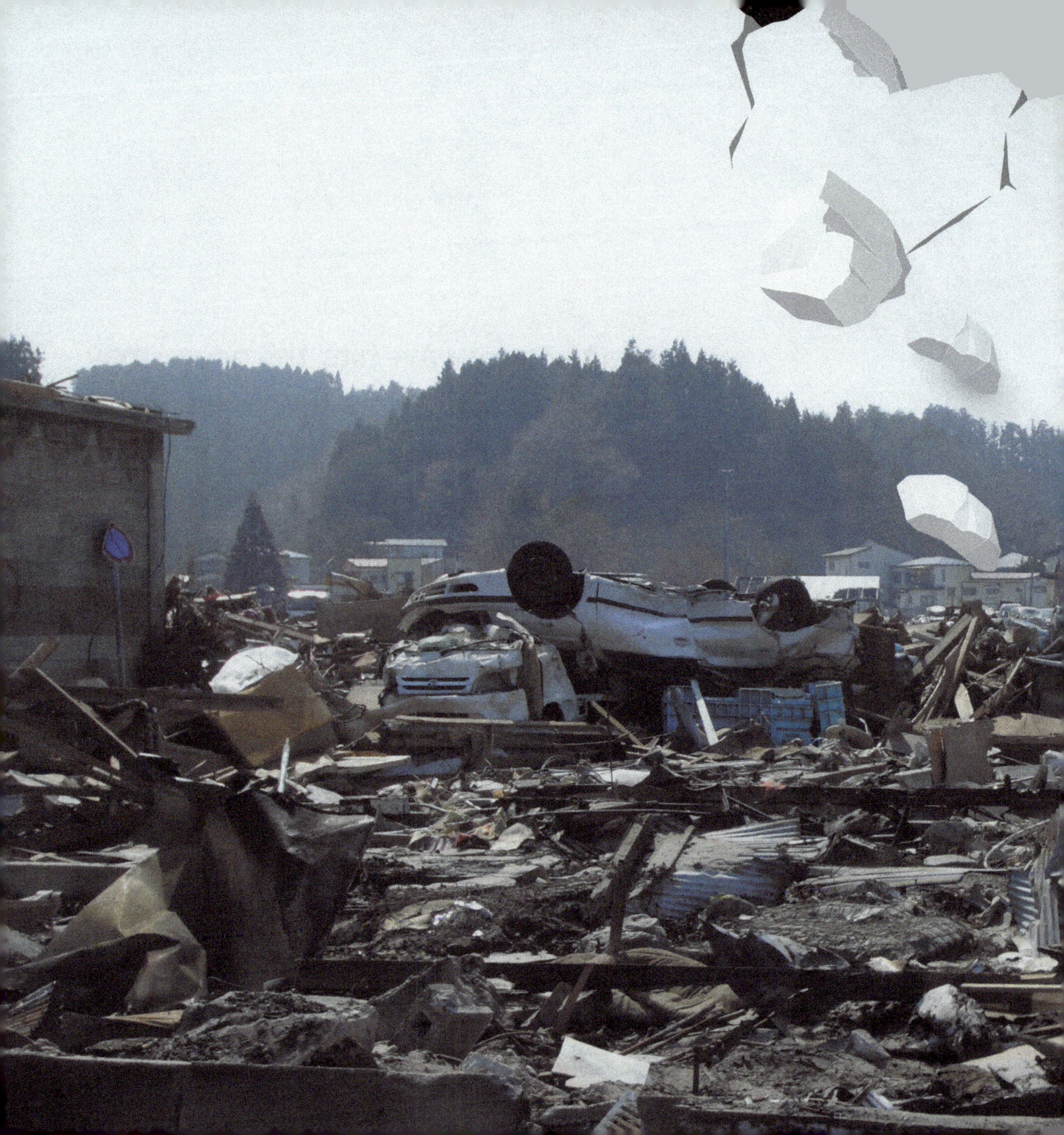

Summary

Earthquakes are caused by energy waves moving through the earth. Some earthquakes are very small and happen all the time. Others are very strong and destroy buildings and open cracks in the earth. The study of earthquakes is called Seismology.

There are two main kinds of seismic waves. Body waves travel inside the earth. The two types are primary and secondary waves. Surface waves move over the surface of the earth. The two types are Love waves and Rayleigh waves. The starting point of an earthquake is the focus. The epicenter is where surface waves spread out from.

Most earthquakes start near the boundaries of tectonic plates. Transform boundaries move past each other in opposite directions. Converging boundaries move toward each other. Diverging boundaries move away from each other. Faults are cracks in the earth's crust that you can see.

When two plates stick together, pressure builds until they break apart. This is what causes an earthquake to start.

Earthquakes can be measured using a seismograph. Seismographs measure the strength of an earthquake, how long it lasted, and which direction its waves were moving in by marking lines on a piece of paper. The strength of an earthquake is called its magnitude.

The Mercalli Scale measures how strong an earthquake was by looking at how much damage it caused. The Richter Scale measures how strong an earthquake was by using a mathematical equation.

Tsunamis are giant waves caused by earthquakes near or under the ocean. They are hard to predict because they look very small until they reach the coast. If you see the water disappearing from the beach, you will only have a few minutes to get to higher ground where it is safe.

Now that you know all about earthquakes and tsunamis, you'll probably want to know more about the earth. Try reading **Peeling The Earth Like An Onion: Earth Composition** - Geology Books for Kids | Children's Earth Sciences Books.

Visit

www.speedypublishing.com/

To view and download free content on your favorite subject and browse our catalog of new and exciting books for readers of all ages.